Respect Virus

How to Create a Contagious Culture of Respect

DIANE WINDINGLAND

ISBN-10: 0983007888
ISBN-13: 978-0-9830078-8-3

Contents

Introduction

What if respect were a virus? Would you help spread it?

Attitudes are contagious. They are contagious because others react to actions driven by attitudes. Disrespect can spread and create a toxic environment, or respect can be passed from person to person to create a healthy environment.

Respect costs little, but the benefits at work and in your personal life are priceless. Imagine how a positive, respectful work culture could enhance productivity where you work. Imagine how respectful conversation at home could reduce conflict and enhance your family relationships.

If you can imagine it, you can create it.

This book will give you practical strategies and actions you can use right away to create a culture of respect.

"Treating people with respect and valuing them is a universal language. Culture trumps strategy." — Howard Schultz, Starbucks' CEO

Here are a few questions you might have that are answered in this book:

If I just apply the Golden Rule, isn't that good enough?

How can I reduce misunderstandings that lead to conflict?

What are some quick ways I can engage with people and show respect?

How can I make requests without sounding bossy?

How can I move communication from gridlock to dialogue?

How can I criticize with kindness?

It is my hope that the respect virus will spread far and wide and that you will be a carrier!

1. Be Considerate (Platinum Plus Rule)

Being considerate is more than just mere politeness. It means taking the focus off of yourself and considering others' perspectives, treating people as they would want to be treated.

I learned this the hard way, years ago, as my husband and I were driving home from visiting his parents. "You know, my mom is mad at you," said my husband.

"What? Why?"

"You didn't help with the dishes."

"I offered to help," I said, "but she said 'No.'"

"You only asked once," he said. "You have to ask three times, and insist on the third time."

"Are you kidding me?"

"No. That's just how she does it—refusing the first few offers of help, but giving in when you insist."

I was speechless for a moment. I felt bad that I had let my mother-in-law down. I felt misunderstood. I had offered to help with the dishes, but I respected that it was her house and that she had the right to do things her way, which might include me not helping. Thus, I accepted her "no" at face value.

I had treated my mother-in-law the way that I would want to be treated. I had applied the Golden Rule.

The Golden Rule: *Do unto others as you would have them do unto you.*

Many people consider the Golden Rule to be at the root of respect.

But there is a problematic assumption in the Golden Rule: "Other people are like me." The problem is that how you want to be treated may not be how other people want to be treated.

Enter the Platinum Rule.

The Platinum Rule: *Do unto others as they would have you do unto them.*

The Platinum Rule, an age-old concept, was popularized by author and motivational speaker Tony Alessandra. This rule means that we should treat other people the way they want to be treated, not the way we want to be treated.

The Platinum Rule is more empathetic than the Golden Rule. And in the case of my mother-in-law and the dishes, after I realized how the "dish game" was played, I changed my behavior to treat my mother-in-law the way she wanted to be treated.

The Platinum Rule is an improvement on the Golden Rule, but I see three main challenges with the Platinum Rule:

1. How people want to be treated may be in conflict with your values/morals.
2. How people want to be treated may be harmful to them.
3. How people want to be treated is limited by their own imagination.

For example, if a panhandler approaches you for money, the Platinum Rule would dictate that you give him some money. However, it might be against your values to give money to panhandlers. You might think that giving him money could be harmful, if he uses it to buy alcohol. Or you might have something even better than money that you could give him, like a job.

Thus, I propose the Platinum Plus Rule.

The Platinum Plus Rule: *Treat other people the way their best selves would want your best self to treat them.*

Perhaps your best self doesn't want to give money because that is in conflict with your values or you think giving money directly could result in harm. At the same time, your best self respects the humanity of the person in front of you. What you can do then is explore other options (offering to get some food, talking a little bit with the person to determine how you could help in a way that would be mutually agreeable, or even respectfully saying "no").

The challenge is to get outside of your own head. Try to zoom out of your own perspective and look at a situation from the perspective of the other person, or even that of an impartial observer, to get the big picture.

2. Play Perspective Chairs: The 3-Chair Method

Quick. Stop for two seconds and try this: draw a capital letter E on your forehead with your finger.

OK. I'll give you a pass if you are in a crowded office or a coffee shop and don't want to look silly. But if not, take the index finger of your dominant hand and trace the outline of a capital letter E on your forehead before reading further.

Now, think about your E.

In this well-known experiment, the way you draw the E reveals whether you are a person who tends to take the perspective of others. If you drew the E so that you can read it yourself, with the open side of the E pointing to your right (making it backwards for others), you tend not to consider another's point of view.

So what's the big deal if you fail to take another's perspective into account?

Lack of perspective-taking can create challenges both in your personal life (marriage, kids) and in your business life, especially in dealing with conflict.

According to Francesca Gino, author of *Sidetracked: Why Our Decisions Get Derailed, and How We Can Stick to the Plan*, the failures of perspective-taking are many:

1. We overestimate the extent to which others share our attitudes and feelings.

2. We believe that others have more access to our internal states than they actually do.

3. We tend to use ourselves as a standard when evaluating others.

4. We draw on our own experiences when evaluating others.

5. We suffer from the "curse of knowledge" and have a hard time remembering that others do not have the same access to information and knowledge that we do.

I often recall a story told by Stephen Covey in his book, *The 7 Habits of Highly Effective People*. Mr. Covey was riding the subway one day when a man and his children boarded. The man sat in the train staring off into space while the children were acting up. The father made no attempt to control his unruly children and finally, extremely annoyed by the man's poor parenting skills, Covey mentioned to the father that his children were bothering him and the other passengers. The father replied that the children's mother had just died and he didn't know how to handle the situation. That revelation caused Covey to have a paradigm shift in how he viewed the situation. He got a window into the father's interpretation of the situation.

After years of rigorous research (well, make that "occasional observation and personal frustration"), I have developed a simplified model of interpersonal communication. I call it the Mickey Mouse Theory of Interpersonal Communication.

This theory answers basic questions about why we have conflict and misunderstandings. Here is my super-scientific graphical representation of the theory (I'll bet you can see how it got its name):

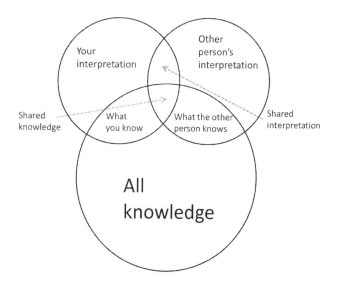

Note that I have given more visual weight to people's interpretation of knowledge than the actual knowledge they possess. The reason is because I believe most of our misunderstandings and conflict stem from differing interpretations, especially interpretations of intent. It is all too easy to jump to conclusions about another person's intent. Have you ever had someone completely misjudge your intent? I know I have. Why does that happen? It happens because the other person has interpreted your intent through his or her own filters based on experience, personality, gender, culture, and so on. We all view the world through our own filters, our framework of understanding.

How can this model help you in your communications? First, remember that you don't have all the information, and neither does the other person. Second, know that your interpretation of the information can be completely different than the other person's. Third, be very cautious about assuming the other person's intent. If you must assume, assume a positive intent. Better yet, instead of assuming, probe for understanding. Ask questions.

So, how can you get better at perspective-taking?

One way is to focus on facts, not assumptions.

A misunderstood person does not feel respected. Most misunderstandings stem from people making bad assumptions.

Here's an example that happened to my husband, Kim, at work when he was a young engineer in his 20s:

Manager: "How long have you lived in this country?"

Kim: "I grew up here."

Manager: "Well, why don't you learn English?"

Ouch. The manager assumed that my husband had poor grammar because he didn't "learn English." The problem was that my husband was hearing impaired, because of an unfortunate encounter with a firecracker when he was six. He didn't speak correctly because he didn't hear correctly. It would have been more respectful for the manager to focus on the facts, such as saying (in a private conversation), "Communicating effectively is an important part of working with people. I notice when you speak that you sometimes leave the ends off words. Were you aware of this?"

A second way to get better at perspective-taking is to use a mental technique I call "Perspective Chairs."

Imagine sitting in each of three chairs of perspective:

1. Your own perspective
2. The other party's perspective
3. An impartial observer's perspective

Sitting in your own chair, or having your own perspective, is easy.

Sitting in the other party's chair, or taking the other person's perspective, is harder. You don't really know all that they know. You don't really know their inner state (maybe something happened prior to your meeting that has affected their emotional state). You don't know how their interpretation of your shared knowledge might differ. So, the first step is realizing that you don't know everything. The second step is seeking to understand. Let go of your assumptions, or bring them out into the open so they can be addressed.

Listen and ask questions. Try to put yourself in their shoes (or chair, in this case).

Sitting in an impartial observer's chair, or getting outside of the situation and taking the perspective of an impartial observer, is perhaps the most difficult. But, in doing so, you are more likely to get the big picture of a situation. In the book *Decisive: How to Make Better Choices in Life and Work*, the authors, brothers Chip and Dan Heath, suggest "zooming out" to get an outside view before making a decision. The same concept can be applied to thinking about interpersonal communication. By zooming out, you take the view of how the situation appears to others. You can even ask yourself what another person, a person whom you respect, would say or how they would act in the situation.

An example of using perspective chairs:

A while back, some friends came over for me to video a promo for a website. I'm not a professional; I just had the equipment. As I thought about how the background of the video would look, I thought that my apartment would be too busy a background, so I suggested we go to the party room of my apartment complex, which had darker walls and upscale decor. When it wasn't specifically reserved, it was open for any resident to use.

When we got to the party room, which was next to the apartment management office, one of the managers was talking to a prospective renter in the room, so we waited just outside the door until the manager said, "Let me get this paperwork copied and then I'll show you around." The manager left, and the prospective renter remained in the room. I figured that she would be leaving soon, so my friends and I entered the room and went to the far end. I set up my tripod and camera and did a couple of trial shoots until the manager came back and talked with the prospective renter for a few more minutes, during which time my friends and I chatted quietly. After the manager left with the prospective renter, we did two more takes (only 30 seconds each), and for the second take, I asked one of my friends to close the door to the room, to cut down on outside noise. As we finished up and I was showing the last take to one of my friends, a different apartment manager came into the room and approached us, looking fairly upset.

"What are you doing?" she asked.

"Shooting a short video for a friend's website," I said.

"You can't close the door and you can't video without permission," she said.

She added something like, "You have to get permission to use footage of this room. Plus, you have to pay for rental."

This was an opportunity to practice the "three chairs method."

My chair/perspective: My initial thoughts were: *What's the big deal? We were in the room for 5 minutes. The door was closed for less than a minute. I need permission to video a wall with a fake plant? Pay rent for 5 minutes when I live here? Really?*

Her chair/perspective: Now, I don't know exactly what her perspective was, but I could try to guess. I noticed that she seemed really upset, more so than I would expect for what I considered to be a relatively small infraction. So, my first thought was that arguing with her might be a bad idea, if she was emotional. Maybe there was something that happened right before this incident that caused her to be in a bad mood. Maybe they had a bad experience with someone videoing in the party room. Maybe they were concerned about managing impressions of the apartment complex. Perhaps my entering the room before the prospective renter had left was bad manners. Perhaps closing the door made them feel I was overstepping my bounds as a renter when I hadn't paid for exclusive use of the room.

Impartial observer chair/perspective: Management was upset. Diane and friends were surprised by management being upset. This might have been avoided if Diane and friends had waited until no one was in the room, or if Diane had asked permission (or if management had clearly defined and posted regulations). Because this was likely a "small potatoes" issue in the long term, and in order not to damage the renter/landlord relationship, de-escalation of the conflict would be a wise course of action.

This is how I replied, given the quick game of "perspective chairs" I had just played in my head:

"I'm sorry. I didn't know I needed permission. We were here for just a few minutes, and the door was only closed a very short time. The only part of the room that was in the video was that wall and the plant." (I explained my position without being defensive, to try to get her to see a little of my perspective.)

"Well, you do need to get permission," she said.

"OK. I'll know that for next time. I'm sorry, I didn't even think about it."

We parted on cordial terms. How do you think the conversation would have gone if I had spoken solely from my perspective?

Take a moment before you react to a situation to "sit in another chair."

I'm not suggesting that you never try to interpret a person's behavior.

Although behavior is subject to misinterpretation, it can provide clues to people's motivations. Generally, people will behave in ways that they think will achieve a desired outcome, revealing what is important to them.

A manager berates his direct reports for missing a deadline. What is the motivation for doing so? Fear for his own job? Desire to be in control? A recognizable pattern may develop.

The challenge is that there are often competing outcomes. For example, a working parent's top priority might be his family. Earning money to provide for that family is a supporting priority, but it typically requires long hours away from the family. The working parent faces a role conflict. How does his behavior reveal motivations? Perhaps the employee copes by texting with his kids or by leaving early for special events.

You can observe this pattern and know that family time is a motivator.

Be observant, but be careful not to assume too much.

Of course, to truly be considerate, to treat other people as they would want to be treated, you have to get to know people both generally and specifically.

The Respect Virus

3. Get to Know People

Learning about people and how to get along with them generally is a critical part of a professional development plan. Books, classes, websites, and assessments abound to help you better understand people.

On-boarding an employee or a client is the most opportune and natural time to ask questions that reveal motivations and personality types. Use a client questionnaire or an employee survey. Consider formal assessments, such as the DISC assessment (the DISC personality test measures four factors of personality: Dominance, Influence, Steadiness, and Compliance). But don't let your assessment be a "one-and-done" assessment. People change. Needs change. Motivations change. How often should you assess? Well, that depends on the situation. One clue that you aren't doing assessments often enough is your retention rate—are your clients or employees leaving you at a higher rate than the industry standard?

Of course, if you merely assess or survey and then don't do anything with that information, then not only have you wasted everyone's time but you also risk looking like someone who has a checklist mentality: you're just going through the motions.

Also, don't limit the assessment to other people! Try taking a simple assessment to understand your own personality. Just for fun, I took one of the many free DISC personality tests online. My results were D (dominance), 37%; I (influence), 42%; S (Steadiness), 16%; and C (Compliance), 5%.

Your scores, especially the highest and lowest scores, can give you some insight as to where you might have some perspective issues. As I scored very low on compliance, I might, for example, butt heads with someone on sticking to rules. What I might see as an efficient way to get something done (by circumventing rules) might seem risky to someone with a higher compliance score.

Getting to know yourself and getting to know others through assessments can give you insights quickly, but assessments don't take the place of getting to know people personally.

That kind of knowledge can best be obtained by spending time with them. It can be as simple as stopping by someone's desk (MBWA–Management By Walking Around) instead of emailing them or texting them. Or get out of the office and have a "walking meeting." A little change of scenery and some exercise are bonuses!

The Respect Virus

4. Create a Personal Engagement Plan: 2 Minutes a Day

Engagement is such a buzzword these days. Employee engagement. Customer engagement. Brand engagement. Social media engagement.

Study after study shows that greater engagement leads to greater retention, better satisfaction, better health, and higher profits.

If engagement is so good, what are you doing personally, every day, to increase engagement at work or in your business?

Engagement can be not only part of an overall organizational engagement strategy but also part of your personal engagement strategy. Engaging personally, connecting with people one-on-one, and creating moments of connection build up an emotional bank account, which can grow your business or your career. It also can create a cushion of loyalty when times get tough.

Isn't that worth two minutes a day?

Try out some of the following ideas for your personal engagement plan.

Chit Chat
Really. You can start talking about the weather, even. Start with something you both have in common.

Things in common = similarity → increased connection.

Try this simple, yet effective, small talk technique:

a. Observe. Make a comment on something that you and the other person can both observe or that you have in common (event, situation, something you see, etc.). It doesn't need to be witty.

b. Transition with a reveal (*optional*). Make a transition comment that relates #a (your observation) to #c (the question) by revealing a tidbit of information about yourself. You can often skip the transition, but by revealing a tidbit of information about yourself, you foster a sense of connection.

c. Ask. Ask a related open-ended question. An open-ended question is one that can't be answered with a one-word reply. It doesn't even have to be a question, but can be a statement that encourages an extended reply, such as "Tell me about..."

Closed-ended question: "How many children do you have?"

Open-ended question/statement: "Tell me about your family."

d. Comment. Follow up with a comment relevant to their response.

e. Ask another question and continue a little back and forth chit chat.

For example, let's say you are walking by someone's desk and you notice a family picture.

Observe: "What a good-looking family!"

Transition with a reveal: "That reminds me of when my kids were little."

Ask: "What do you like to do for family fun?" (Response: "We like to go camping.")

Comment: "Camping! That's a great way to bond as a family."

Ask another question: "What was your favorite camping trip?"

To extend the moment of connection, take note of some details of the conversation to bring up at a later time. I know I feel more connected with people who remember some details about me or what we talked about. For my business clients, I record details of conversations on a Customer Relationship Management (CRM) tool and add scheduled tasks to remind me to touch base.

For example, I was coaching a client on a presentation and knew that her presentation was going to be in a week, on Friday. I put a task in my CRM tool to send her an email on Thursday wishing her well on her presentation. She told me twice, once in email and once in person, how much she appreciated my brief words of encouragement.

Make Personal Gestures
When you show a personal interest in people, you show that you care. Stopping at someone's desk, touching base on the phone, or sending a personal email, text, or social media message are a few quick ways to show that the person is important to you.

Be on the lookout for "thinking of you" opportunities as you come across useful information. Send a link to something you know they would find useful, with a little explanation as to why you thought of them.

When you are first getting to know an employee or a client, if it is appropriate to your business, taking them out to coffee or lunch, away from work, can be a great opportunity to break the ice and start building a relationship.

Invite Them to Something You Are Already Going To

- Meals. You have to eat. Why not use that time to build relationships?

- Events/Activities. Do you share an interest? Why not invite them to join you?

- Volunteer effort for a charitable cause that both you and they care about.

- Meetings, if appropriate.

Use Multiple Modes of Communication

In-person is great but not always practical. What other ways does the person communicate? Phone. Text. Email. Skype. Google Hangouts. Chat. Direct messages on Twitter. Facebook or LinkedIn. A quick video. Or go old school and send something snail mail. Just make sure that you aren't forcing other people to communicate in ways they don't want to.

You never know where attempting moments of connection will lead you! A few years ago, I did an assignment for a class that required doing an exercise on someone's website. I was so impressed with the exercise that I blogged about it and then sent a link to that blog post to the creator of the exercise. She was pleased that I saw value in the exercise and that I promoted its use. From there, we connected on social media sites, email, phone, and Skype. We eventually co-authored a book together. Several months after the book was published, we met in person for the first time.

Respond in a Timely Manner

That last one, timely response, is a deal-breaker for me. When someone doesn't respond to my emails, it makes me feel like I'm not very important to them. Of course, I try to give people the benefit of the doubt, realizing that my email might have gotten trapped in their spam filter or that their response time is just slower (personally, I try to get back to people within 24 hours in most cases). Even if your complete response will take a while, at least get back with people to let them know you received the email and will get back with them by a certain date.

Show Sincere Appreciation

Having a positive-to-negative ratio of at least three positives to every one negative will increase people's productivity, according to researcher Barbara Fredrickson.

But don't just say "thank you." Effective praise is timely, sincere, specific, and shows significance.

EP (Effective Praise) = TS^3

Timely = as soon as reasonably possible. A once-a-year performance review is not enough.

Sincere = from the heart, not manipulative and not just a perfunctory "thank you."

Specific = what specifically was observed. A "good job" statement is not specific.

Significant = show the significant impact the action had.

When possible, make your appreciation public. Public appreciation (at a meeting, for example) not only lets you express your gratitude but also elevates the person in the eyes of others.

Try keeping a praise log to record positive performance. Here's an Excel example:

	A	B	C	D	E	F	G
1			Praise Log				
2	Date	name	observed behavior	impact	feedback	feedback date	notes
3							
4							
5							
6							
7							

Encourage others to catch someone doing something well! Where my husband works, they have an informal program that allows anyone to recognize anyone else with a small reward (a gift card).

Practice Small Acts of Kindness

A cookie can make all the difference. A few years ago, I attended a convention in Las Vegas in which the business meeting dragged on and on. I sat next to an associate who started getting a little irritated. Let's call her "Miss Crabby Pants."

Maybe Miss Crabby Pants' attitude had something to do with staying up all night playing blackjack. It was Vegas, after all.

I decided I needed to grab a bite to break the monotony and to get a little break from Miss Crabby Pants, so I headed for the overpriced coffee vendor near the hotel lobby. As I stood in line, I noticed huge (6-inch), chewy-looking chocolate chip cookies. They were only $1.50, a comparative bargain. Inspired initially by the low cost, and later by the thought that a chocolate chip cookie could act as a "happy pill," I bought three cookies and three waters (for myself, Miss Crabby Pants, and her husband). Had I known that a simple cookie could bring about a complete change in attitude, I would have acted sooner. Miss Crabby Pants vanished upon merely seeing the little treat. In her place appeared, almost magically, Miss "Life Is Wonderful and So Are You!"

Do you have a "Miss Crabby Pants" at work? What if you practiced a small act of kindness? Even if it didn't change the person's attitude, wouldn't you feel better for having tried? You never know when your smile or your kind word might be the one that makes someone's day.

The Respect Virus

5. Share Power

It was a lesson I learned playing tug-of-war in gym class: None of us is as powerful as all of us.
Even the weakest of us had power that could make a difference. Nobody had to "empower" us.
Empowerment is a concept that on the surface sounds good, until you really think about what it means. The prefix "em" means to "put into." To empower people is to put power into them, to enable them to do something. Well, that's better than complete domination, but it is still top-down control.
What if companies went beyond mere empowerment and instead maximized everyone's power?
Not power to dominate. Power to liberate. Power to create. Power to share.
Shared power leads to shared knowledge. Shared knowledge leads to better performance. Better performance leads to better results.
Here are a few ways to get started with power sharing:

Ask. Don't always be the solution provider. Two powerful questions to ask are "What do you want?" (asked respectfully, with no eye rolling) and "What are your choices?"

Share information and resources. Provide information and resources (including training) that others may not even realize can help them provide their best value.

Share roles and responsibilities. Consider co-facilitation of meetings, for example. Some roles and responsibilities could even be rotated, which will also deepen empathy and understanding among team members. Or you could let someone who reports to you at work attend a meeting in your place.

Share reasons. Better yet, develop the reasons "why" together. People buy into what they help create.

Make empathetic requests. Nobody likes to be told to do things, even if you say "please" at the start. The secret to having people feel respected when you make a request (and also one of the secrets to getting them to comply) is to couch the request in terms of their point of view, empathizing with their situation, explaining the importance of your request, and asking for buy-in. So instead of saying: "Christine, can you please organize the prospective membership database in the next month?" (even with the "please" it still sounds a bit bossy).

Try saying: "Christine, I can only imagine how busy you are having to deal with all the requests from the newly elected officers" (empathetic to Christine's point of view), "but our recruitment kick-off is coming up soon and we need to get all the prospective members' information organized" (importance of request). "We need you to get that information together in the next month. Is that reasonable?" (requesting buy-in).

Be a little vulnerable. Don't you love being vulnerable? It's hard being vulnerable. Kids are vulnerable. But as we get older, we put on the bulletproof vest of invulnerability. We cinch it tighter for fear that if we open up just a little, we might get shot down. An arrow of judgment might pierce our heart.
But it is when you can be a little vulnerable with people that you can build trust and connect. Sometimes being vulnerable is admitting responsibility for a mistake. Other times being vulnerable is sharing our own challenges.

A few years ago, I had coffee with a new acquaintance. As we sat at across the table from each other, we shared a little about ourselves. He shared how he had been out of work for a while and was getting most of his food at a food shelf. I could see the guarded expression on his face, the invisible wall between us. I knew he wondered if I would judge him, if I would think poorly of him for being out of work.

I decided to be strategically vulnerable.

I shared with him that I knew how he felt, because just two years earlier, we had been dealing with a failed business. Just two years earlier, not only had I gotten food at a food shelf, I'd gotten my kids' Christmas gifts there too. But it was temporary. Hard, but temporary—as it would be for him, too. Tough times don't last. Tough people do.

The wall came down. His face relaxed. He leaned in. We connected. And I began to discover what made him tick.

Taking off the bulletproof vest might be hard. It might be scary. It might just change your relationships.

Create an inclusive culture. Treat people fairly regardless of race, color, political views, gender, age, and so on. Make diversity training a part of your work environment. Focus also on similarities—however people are different, they are more alike than different. People who can see similarities despite differences are more likely to like and respect each other. Team-building activities can encourage bonding and create shared experiences, which increase feelings of similarity.

Beyond diversity issues, freely share information and resources, where confidentiality is not an issue.

"In the past a leader was a boss. Today's leaders must be partners with their people … they no longer can lead solely based on positional power." –Ken Blanchard

The Respect Virus

6. Move from Gridlock to Dialogue: Stop

"My project has the potential to be a big win for the company," said Dave, a project manager. "I need Asha and Jake full time for at least the next three weeks."

"Well, a bird in the hand is worth two in the bush!" said Tom, another project manager. "Raven [Tom's project] is with our current biggest customer. Bluebird [Dave's project] can wait."

His lips a thin line and his jaw hard set, Dave glared at Tom across the conference table.

Tom's eyes narrowed and returned a cold, steely stare. Neither project manager was going to budge. They had locked horns over the issue of shared resources, specifically the test engineers who supported both of their projects. The company didn't have the budget to hire more test engineers, so Tom and Dave were gridlocked in what was essentially a battle for dominance.

Their boss, who didn't believe in micromanaging his project managers, could have been like Solomon and split the two test engineers, but that would have left both project managers feeling resentful, so he told them to "figure it out."

Have you ever felt like you were butting heads?

To stop butting heads and to move from gridlock to dialogue when you face an impasse, the first step is to stop.

When people argue or are at a frustrating gridlock, emotions can be high and cause an automatic physical stress response, the fight-or-flight response. The fight-or-flight response keeps us from danger by making us want to fight or run away. Sometimes, the threat can be so overwhelming that a "freeze response" (deer in the headlights) is triggered.

With fight, flight, or freezing up, you may experience increased heart rate and respiration, red or pale face, tense muscles, rapid speech, sweating, tunnel vision, and more. What you won't experience is your best quality thinking. Stress can alter and disrupt the executive function of the brain, which affects memory, problem solving, and decision making.

Stop, take a break from looking at the issue the same way, and give yourself a chance to calm down, reflect, and better examine the problem.

Here are some ways to "Stop":

Take a break. *"I think we need a little break."* Depending on the circumstances, you could suggest anything from a short "bio" break (15 minutes) to a few hours, or to another day. For longer breaks, suggest that all parties do some "homework" to examine the true needs, which may involve getting more information and considering possible alternatives.

Move on to something else. *"We seem to be stuck on this issue. Let's move on to another issue and come back to this one later."* Ideally, the new issue you choose will be one that you can have more conversation around. Elimination of conflict isn't the goal, as long as the conversation is moving forward!

Reframe: Stop the trajectory. *"Let's take a look at this from a completely different angle."* Shift the direction of the gridlocked discussion. In the example of the two project managers gridlocked over which of their projects more deserved the test engineers, Dave might have reframed the discussion. *"Let's take a look at this from a completely different angle. How would a delay impact each of our customers?"*

New eyes. Stop trying to resolve it yourself. Get someone else's perspective. *"I think getting X's perspective might give us some insights."* You could have a mutually agreed upon person give his or her perspective, or you could each pick someone to give a perspective. Ideally, the person giving a perspective would be one the other party respects.

7. Move from Gridlock to Dialogue: Listen

Many people appear to be listening, when in fact they are just waiting for their turn to talk. To uncover someone's motivations, you need to practice active, reflective listening. To ensure that you understand the other person, try this approach:

Listen fully, without interrupting, except to reflect back or to clarify. Resist debate until you have fully understood. Most gridlock occurs because both parties feel they have needs and expectations that aren't likely to be met if they "give in." Try to put yourself in the other person's shoes as you listen to try to understand those needs and expectations. Realize that you don't know everything. There may be hidden issues.

In the earlier example, perhaps Dave had a poor performance review and knows that effectively managing this project is critical to his career. Tom may not know this, and Dave is unlikely to tell him. However, Tom might notice from Dave's body language, voice inflection, and choice of words *("My project...", "I need...")* that Dave is personally very invested.

Here are some ways to "Listen":

Focus. This is not the time to be checking your email or texting. Nor is it the time to be mentally formulating your response. Listening isn't simply waiting for your turn to talk. Listen with your ears and eyes. Your ears hear more than words. Ears pick up tone of voice and pauses. Your eyes read facial expressions and body language, which will enhance meaning greatly (think about those times that someone has misinterpreted your email, because they couldn't see your face or hear your tone of voice).

Listen reflectively. If you want to make sure that you understand a particular point, reflect it back (using the same words or paraphrasing), and check that this is really what was meant. Visually reflect back by nodding. Nod when you agree, but also when you understand what someone is saying. Nodding will encourage people to talk more. You can even give verbal nods of encouragement with sounds like "ahhh…" and "umhmm."

- Ask clarifying questions if something is not clear.

- Test for understanding.
    - Start out with a lead-in phrase, such as "So, it sounds like…" or, "So, what I hear you saying is…" A lead-in phrase

is a verbal cue to the other person that you are going to reflect back your understanding.

- Restate (paraphrase, summarize) facts, feelings, opinions, and so on.

- Ask for confirmation (use phrases like "Is that right?" or "Is that what you meant?").

Limit interruptions. Limit interruptions to those that enhance understanding, such as reflecting back or asking clarifying questions. Don't jump in to make a point before you have fully understood the other person's point.

Take notes. Taking brief notes will aid your concentration, give you some points to ask for clarification on, and make the other person feel like you are taking them seriously.

Avoid communication stoppers.
- Don't use negative nonverbals such as eye rolling, head shaking, and sighing.

- Don't use stop-sign statements. These are statements that are like a big red stop sign.

(Examples: "You're wrong" or "That's stupid.") If the other person keeps talking after you have thrown out a stop-sign statement, they risk getting run over and so will usually stop talking, or they will escalate the conversation into a no-win conflict. If you feel the urge to say something like "you're wrong," ask a question instead (in a friendly "we're-all-in-this-together" tone). "I don't quite understand how that will work... Can you show me how...?"

Make it safe. If danger alarms are going off, people will revert to survival mode. They will be motivated most by that which ensures survival. Other motivations will be suppressed. Reduce the environment and attitudes that create fear (here is a very partial list):

- Public criticism
- Emotional outbursts
- Adversarial relationships
- Disrespectful communication
- Pointing fingers, but being unwilling to accept responsibility for mistakes
- Withholding important information or resources

8. Move from Gridlock to Dialogue: Clarify

Clarification, at the most basic level, involves asking questions to gain a clear understanding. But not just any kind of questions will do. Here are some examples of counterproductive questions:

Bad Questions
- How can you be so stupid? (degrading and emotionally charged)
- Did I put that in terms simple enough for you? (condescending)
- Are you trying to pull the wool over my eyes? (aggressive)
- Are you done yet? (impatient and closed-ended)

Some questions aren't "bad." They are just "tricky" (psychologically leading). An example:
"Do you and your manager work well together?" (subtly suggests there could be problems).

Don't Interrogate
If you want to get people talking, ask them easy, open-ended questions or probing statements (questions or statements that encourage more than a one-word

answer) and build on their answers, digging a little deeper.

Try not to ask questions in rapid-fire, interrogation style. Build rapport by commenting on what they say, especially if you can point out any similarities that you have (the more people see you as like them, the more they will like, trust, and open up to you).

There are better questions to ask. Ask questions that display respect.

An alternative to the question "Do you and your manager work well together?" might be to rephrase it: "Tell me about your working relationship with your manager." ("Tell me" can encourage conversation even more than a question.)

Some ways to "Clarify":

Five W's and one H: *Who, What, When, Where, Why, and How. The Five W's and One H* give you a framework for question categories. For example: Who is responsible? What are the goals? When is it due? Where does it go? Why is this important? How is it used?

Clarify the scope of the issue. What's the problem? How big is it? What does it affect? What are the likely limitations in solving the problem (time, money, resources, technology)? Is there a process?

Clarify the method of issue analysis. Are you just going to talk about the issue or will a formal format or method be used? Will you drill down by asking "Why?" repeatedly? Will you use a SWOT analysis (Strengths, Weaknesses, Opportunities, Threats)? Lists? Mind maps? Cause and effect diagrams? Problem tree?

Clarify the criteria. What are the critical criteria for making decisions? Are there specifications to meet? A deadline? How will solution alternatives be evaluated? What is the set of required or mutually acceptable criteria?

Clarify facts versus opinions. Facts can be checked. Opinions can be supported by facts. Do you have enough relevant facts to form well-supported opinions?

The Respect Virus

9. Move from Gridlock to Dialogue: Agree

Find a point of agreement. In a gridlocked conversation, people can become so entrenched in their opposing viewpoints that they fail to see the many areas of agreement. A small point of agreement can lead to an avalanche of agreement.

Zoom off. If you can get other people saying "yes" on other issues ("*move on to something else*") you not only get a break from the issue at hand, you also build positive lean-forward momentum.

Zoom out. You can zoom out of the situation and look at it more globally, finding agreement on the "big picture" or the company's mission and values and then zoom it back in to the issue at hand.

Zoom in. If you can get them saying "yes" on minor points (or even points that are not in contention), you change the nature of the discussion and make it easier to come to an agreement.

You can even have a series of easy questions, questions that all have the answer "yes," to move from gridlock to dialogue.

In the example of the two project managers:

Dave: "Tom, we've been butting heads on this issue all week." (Tom nods "yes.")

"Going 'round and 'round is getting us nowhere, right?"

Tom: "You're right on that!" (A second "yes.")

Dave: "It seems the problem boils down to us both wanting the same resources at the same time." (Dave goes for agreement on what the problem is.)

Tom: "That about sums it up." (A third "yes.")

Dave: "So, if we could find a way to use different resources, or the same resources but at different times, then our problem would be solved, right?" (Dave sets up for another way of thinking about the problem.)

Tom: "Yeah, but I don't see how that would happen." (A fourth "yes," qualified with skepticism.)

At this point, Tom is opening up to hearing some of Dave's ideas, which might wisely include bringing in a third-party perspective. Gridlock has turned to dialogue.

10. Move from Gridlock to Dialogue: Focus on Solutions

In a gridlocked conversation, the problem often seems to be the other person. You end up in a "You versus Me" battle.

Win or lose, you lose.

If you win, it is a hollow victory if the other person feels resentful and vindictive toward you.

Another approach is "Both of Us versus The Problem." It's not you versus me, it's both of us versus the problem. This has the advantage of encouraging cooperation and is a useful mind shift. An even more productive mind shift is "We Find a Solution."

It's not that understanding problems isn't important. But as humans, we have a tendency to get mired in the problems. The reason we tend to focus on problems rather than solutions is that our brains are prediction machines, continually trying to predict outcomes of actions while at the same time trying to minimize risk and maximize reward. Problems are often based on past experience, so it is easier to focus on them. Solutions lie in the uncertain future.

Here are a few ways to get started on focusing on solutions:

Simplify the situation by stating the major clear goals (don't start with a comprehensive, detailed list).

Look at the big picture. Think whole to parts. Consider the big picture first and then the relevant details.

Take small steps. Act parts to whole. Solve small parts, in small steps. Consider trial solutions to gather data as to feasibility.

Minimize problems with the possible solution at first. Give the solution a chance to grow in people's imaginations before you allow people to snipe at it ("let's focus on how this can work before we pick it apart").

In the example with the project managers, Dave might have proposed the following trial solution:

Dave: "Tom, would you be willing to try an idea for three days? Asha and Jake are willing to work overtime—to work up to 12 hours a day each, 6 hours for each of our projects. Actually, they both would like the extra money and are OK with working hard for a few weeks. I got the OK from John to try it for a few days, if you are agreeable. He said there would be enough money in the budget to do it for a month, if it works out. Are you willing to try it for three days?"

Tom: "Well, I guess we could try it. It will probably push out the schedule. But for three days … let's do it."

Move your conversations from gridlock to dialogue: Stop. Listen. Clarify. Agree. Focus on Solutions.

"In solving a problem, think whole to parts, but act parts to whole."—Diane Windingland

11. Criticize with Kindness

"You missed a spot!"

"You're leaving the house looking like *that*?"

Criticism. Does anyone truly enjoy receiving criticism? Does anyone truly enjoy giving criticism?

It's hard to criticize without causing anger, hurt, or defensiveness. You could take the ostrich approach and just bury your head in the sand and ignore others' failings. Sometimes that is the best approach, especially for trivial matters. However, just because people don't like being criticized, that doesn't mean we can avoid doing it. If we allow people to continue doing the wrong thing, we build up feelings of resentment. The secret is to criticize with kindness, and sparingly.

To criticize with kindness, consider why, when, and how.

Why Criticize?
First, the **bad** reasons to criticize:
- To hurt someone
- To vent frustrations or anger

- To build up your own ego (it makes you feel superior)

Good reasons to criticize include:
- Helping someone improve—You want to help someone get better.
- Making a necessary change—You want something done differently.
- Initiating a discussion to consider change—You want to start or further discussion.

When to Criticize

Timing is important. Don't criticize when you or the other person is rushed or upset. Typically, you would want to offer criticism in private. Remember the old adage: "Criticize in private, praise in public." Receiving criticism is difficult enough, but having other people witness the event is sheer agony. Allow people to "save face" by criticizing them privately.

Also, make sure that people understand your expectations or standards and how to meet them. Is more training necessary? Do people have the right tools? Take the blame whenever you can. It will soften the criticism and turn it back on yourself. "I don't think I explained clearly enough how to do this…"

How to Criticize

1. Consider your tone of voice, body language, and

attitude. I've learned that you can say almost anything with a warm, genuine smile and not get hit (physically or verbally!).

2. If possible, truthfully admit "I've made the same mistake myself." This phrase does wonders for reducing the air of superiority that accompanies most criticism.

3. Be specific in your criticism. Don't just say, "You did a bad job cleaning the windows." Say something like, "The windows have streaks. Our customers expect clear windows." Try to explain why something needs to change.

4. Do not attack the person; attack the problem.

5. Sandwich the criticism with positive comments.

"Sandwich" Technique

I learned this technique in Toastmasters. Not only does it work for evaluating speeches, but it also works in everyday work and social situations. Sandwich the critical feedback between compliments or positive feedback. People love sincere compliments and positive feedback.

For example, when my daughter was a teenager, she cleaned my home (for pay, of course). At one time, I needed to address an area for improvement.

Compliment: "Clara, you are such a hard worker! You're much better at cleaning than I was at your age."

Gentle Feedback: "You might not have noticed that the lower edge of the shower in the downstairs bathroom gets really dusty. I know it's easy to miss. I'm sure you could just swipe it clean when you're in that area. OK?"

Compliment: "I do really love having you clean my house. Keep up the good work!"

Don't "pop the balloon" with a "but." Notice I don't use the word "but" (or its fancier versions, "however" or "although"). If I had said something like, "You are such a hard worker! You're much better at cleaning than I was at your age, but you missed the lower edge of the shower…" the "but" would negate the compliment. Giving a compliment and then negating it with "but" is like inflating a balloon and then taking a pin and popping it.

When my son was 20 and looking for work, he didn't understand the importance of a first impression. My son's "bed head" might have been appropriate for an indie film but not for looking for a job.

Compliment: "Sean, good choice in clothes! The dark pants and button-down shirt look sharp. They'll make a great first impression."

Gentle Feedback: "You know, I think you could make an even better first impression with your hair groomed to match your clothes."

Compliment: "You look so handsome dressed so nicely!"

When you use the sandwich technique, you may have people feeling glad that you criticized them! Criticize with kindness.

The Respect Virus

12. Advice on Unsolicited Advice

During the "bio-break" at a professional association event, the seasoned professional speaker held up my business card (Small Talk, Big Results) and studied it. Shifting her gaze from the card to me, she said, "You should consider changing your business name. Small talk sounds like small stuff. You need to focus on the big results."

Her large blue eyes locked onto mine, waiting for a response.

My internal conversation, which lasted for about two seconds, went something like this:

Do I disagree and tell her that other professional speakers had told me that it was a catchy business name? Do I agree with her and say, I too, had wondered if the phrase, "small talk" might seem too soft-skill? Wait...why is she telling me this? I didn't ask for her advice. Is she fishing for business? Is this why she asked for my card? (She had told me earlier she was looking at adding on a consultant/coaching aspect to her business.)

I responded with a noncommittal "hmmm."

Reflecting later on the conversation, I felt annoyed.

I hadn't asked for her advice. I didn't even really know the woman. She was merely a professional acquaintance with whom I had exchanged perhaps a dozen words prior to that day. What right did she have to give me unsolicited advice?

Even when someone has the "right" to give unsolicited advice (e.g., mothers-in-law), it doesn't make it any easier to swallow.

"Unsolicited advice is the junk mail of life."
–Bern Williams

As I reflected on the conversation further, I felt pangs of guilty recognition. Shame, shame, shame on me! How many times had I given unsolicited advice?

My poor husband had first been the recipient of my "helpful" advice when, during his business presentations that I sat in on early in our marriage, I would take notes of all his grammar and pronunciation mistakes and hand him the list afterward. Ouch.

Then came my children, whom I homeschooled. Need I say more? Ouch.

And what about the countless times I offered unsolicited advice to people in my professional and volunteer spheres of influence? Ouch.

Humbled by my own guilty conscience, I resolved to approach advice differently. Here's my advice on unsolicited advice:

1. Don't waste your time giving unsolicited advice. People who don't ask for advice are unlikely to listen to it. Of course, this doesn't apply to books! If people read them, they are implicitly asking for advice.

2. If you feel extremely compelled to give unsolicited advice, consider:

> • Your relationship to the recipient. Only give unsolicited advice if you have the respect of the recipient.

> • Asking, "May I give you advice on this?"

> • Sharing information from another source, not giving your own opinion.

> • Positioning your advice as another way to do something, not the only way.

- Not giving advice "after the fact." It's like rubbing salt in the wound.

Of course, you can take my advice…or not.

Conclusion

I hope this book has infected you with the respect virus. I hope you are highly contagious.

Apply the Platinum Plus Rule and treat other people the way their best selves would want your best self to treat them. Use the three-chair technique to zoom out of your own perspective and into another's so that you can reduce misunderstandings that lead to perceived disrespect. Create your own personal engagement plan to get to know people and show respect. Share power, don't just empower. Move from gridlock to dialogue by first stopping and then listening, clarifying, agreeing, and focusing on solutions. Criticize with kindness, and don't generally give unsolicited advice.

The respect virus starts with you. Apply the techniques in this book and you will be well on your way to creating a culture of respect. Share this book with others and you will become a carrier of respect. It's simple, painless, and easy to do. Will you join me in helping to spread the respect virus far and wide? I hope you will.

The Respect Virus

Conclusion

The Respect Virus

Conclusion

The Respect Virus

33560231R00046

Made in the USA
Charleston, SC
18 September 2014